THE POWER OF CHOICE

Bishop C.H. Wright

Copyright © 2018 by Bishop C.H. Wright

All rights reserved. No part of this book may be used or reproduced by any means, graphic, electronic, or mechanical, including photocopying, recording, taping or by any information storage retrieval system without the written permission of the publisher except in the case of brief quotations embodied in critical articles and reviews.

Bishop C.H. Wright/Rejoice Essential Publishing

PO BOX 512
Effingham, SC 29541
www.republishing.org

Copyright © 2018 Bishop C.H. Wright

Scripture quotations marked (NIV) are taken from the Holy Bible, New International Version®, NIV®. Copyright © 1973, 1978, 1984, 2011 by Biblica, Inc.™ Used by permission of Zondervan. All rights reserved.

Scripture quotations taken from the Amplified® Bible (AMP), Copyright © 2015 by The Lockman Foundation. Used by permission. www.Lockman.org

Unless otherwise indicated, Scripture is taken from the King James Version.

All rights reserved.

The Power of Choice/Bishop C.H. Wright

ISBN-10: 1-946756-39-3
ISBN-13: 978-1-946756-39-8
Library of Congress Control Number: 2018951980

Dedication

During some turbulent times in my life and despite the waywardness of my living, God spoke to me and gave me a love for Him and a love for His people.

—Bishop C.H. Wright

TABLE OF CONTENTS

ACKNOWLEDGEMENTS...........ix

INTRODUCTION...............................1

CHAPTER 1:   Choose Life.............5

CHAPTER 2:   Choose A Positive Attitude...12

CHAPTER 3:   Choose Your Influences..............27

CHAPTER 4:   Choosing to Honor.....................36

CHAPTER 5:   Choose Successful Habits....................40

CHAPTER 6:   Choose Wisdom - Make It Your Obsession...............50

CONCLUSION..............................63

ABOUT THE AUTHOR................65

Acknowledgements

I thank God for the gift of Love. I also thank God for my lovely wife, Annie. I am thankful for Elder Moore, Mother Porter, and Bishop Rodgers.

INTRODUCTION

I can remember being a young man and assuming I knew more than most adults including my teachers. By the time I reached 11th grade I decided to drop out of school. I got caught up in the streets and eventually hit rock bottom and it was there- having made bad choice after bad choice- that I finally made a good choice. I chose to look to God and have been looking to Him ever since.

The life that my wife and I are blessed to enjoy today is a far cry from the life that we embarked on as a young couple. I like to tell people that we come from "the other side of the track, behind that track, on the other side of the other track." We don't look like what we've been through!

This book was born out of that season of trusting and working with God to come out of our proverbial Lo Debar. There was no magic potion. It took faith in God, hard work and a lot of good choices. My desire is to teach you what I learned on my journey out.

Many people are quick to act without thoroughly thinking about the effects. Some choices have positive or negative consequences. God has given us the ability to choose between life and death. I will show you how making the right choice or choosing the right activities will lead to a life full of blessings rather than those that will lead to sufferings. After we discuss choosing the right choice, we will cover having a positive attitude. Attitude is the kind of mindset that we have while dealing with our fellow humans. Attitude determines the kind of life we lead. Whether we will be people burdened with sadness or if we will be happy people living according to God's will is also determined by a positive attitude. I have learned that simply having good attitudes can open doors of prosperity for us.

I am passionate about encouraging people from all walks of life to choose their influences wisely. I will share four major lessons I learned about the company we keep. Those who keep bad company will have their good morals corrupted. I urge you not to sit with men who are deceitful. We should avoid making friends with those who are always angry and also stay far from those who are wicked. I also share the revelation that God gave me about choosing to honor. The choices we make over the everyday activities determine the nature of our relationship with God. We take many things for granted such as what we wear or what we eat. I will show you how these things have a significant impact on how we relate to God's will. Our actions and behaviors should honor both God and those that we share our space with.

I have learned many powerful lessons about choosing successful habits. In every success, there is a background of good choices. I urge you to keep dreaming, choose passion over passivity, choose God confidence over self-confidence, know and appreciate our personal limitations, and to hear both sides of a story before making a choice. I empower you to choose wisdom and make it your obsession. Wisdom is the greatest thing and the principle thing in life. Without wisdom, all other choices we make are not valuable to us. Wisdom also includes knowledge and understanding of our world and the ways of God. Wisdom is the foundation of both knowledge and understanding.

CHAPTER 1

CHOOSE LIFE

"I call heaven and earth to record this day against you, that I have set before you life and death, blessing and cursing; therefore choose life, that both thou and thy seed may live." —Deuteronomy 30:19

God gave us a choice between blessings or curses, life or death, and He asks us to choose life. Now this choosing of life is not as simple as choosing to keep living or breathing but rather choosing to make choices that will lead to life and blessings. In Deuteronomy 30, Moses was leaving the children of Israel with instructions for a full and prosperous life: they were to love the Lord, walk in His ways, and to keep His commandments.

Failure to do these things would result in them forfeiting all the blessings that God had spoken concerning them. Many of those who started out with Moses died without ever entering the promised land. Like the children of Israel, we miss out on God's best when we choose to live opposite of His commandments.

One of the greatest examples of choosing life is found in the story of Rahab (Joshua 2). Joshua had sent spies to Jericho, and they came to Rahab's house - Rahab was a harlot so men being in her home was not uncommon. When the King sent for the men, Rahab hid them in the roof and sent the king's men looking in the opposite direction. Her choice to hide the spies could have cost her life, but she did it anyway. The choices we are confronted with are typically not that drastic, but they are still important.

Do you make another debt when your budget is already tight? Do you immediately respond in anger or do you wait and respond in love? Do you tell a lie to save face or be honest and give God an opportunity to work on your behalf? Do you do the thing that you know is wrong and go to the place that you know the saints don't belong or do you stand in your salvation and maintain your integrity? These are some decisions that we are faced with every day and we tend to think they don't matter. But every choice is a step towards life and blessing or death and cursing.

Not only do our choices affect our personal lives, but they also have an effect on our family. Our walk with God can either help or hinder our family as well as those who are connected to us. Let's think about Rahab again. Her decision to hide the spies positioned her to save not only her life, but that of her family.

And Joshua saved Rahab the harlot alive, and her father's household, and all that she had; and she dwelleth in Israel even unto this day; because she hid the messengers, which Joshua sent to spy out Jericho. —-Joshua 6:25

God will pick someone out of a family to be the priest of that family. When that person surrenders to God they are interrupting the cycle of sin throughout that family. As more family members come to know God, a

Godly legacy is being established. I can remember God telling me as a young preacher to go to one of my aunts and talk to her about the way she was living. Although my aunt was in church, she was still 'shacking.'

I was taught that you never get so grown that you can disrespect your elders, so I knew that if I didn't handle this conversation right my aunt just might whip me. I was scared, but I had to obey God, so I went to see her. I finally got around to telling her what God said and I actually made it out of her house without getting hit. That aunt eventually got married and although everyone is not doing everything that they should, there are more family members in the kingdom now than before.

My choice to serve God had a profound effect not just on my bloodline but on that of my wife. We were party people before I got saved. She respected my new life and made sure her family and friends did too. Eventually, she gave her life to the Lord, breaking the cycle of sin in her family as well. We were blessed to lead both of our mothers to the Lord and have seen several of our siblings and their spouses come into the faith. All of our children and their spouses are in the faith, except one, and he is on the way now. Our choice to serve God and govern our home in a Godly way has been a blessing to our family as well as to those who are connected to us.

An example of poor choices effecting future generations is found in the very first story in the bible, the story of Adam and Eve. God gave Adam and Eve a choice of the trees in the Garden of Eden of which they could partake. They chose to eat the fruit from the tree of the knowledge of good and evil. Because of their act of disobedience, sin and death entered the world (Genesis 3:1-24). The moment Eve chose to entertain the serpent, she gave him a foothold in her life. When she, along with Adam, acted on what he said, their choice gave him an all-access pass to their life and future generations.

Genesis 15:5 tells another story of choices affecting future generations. God tells Abram, who is childless, that his seed will outnumber the stars. After much trying Abram's wife becomes discouraged and gives him her maid, Hagar, as a wife (Genesis 16:3). Their doubt in God's promise led them to take matters into their own hands. Their foolish decision led to Hagar bearing Abram's first son Ismael. Years later, Abram, who later was known as Abraham, was blessed with the son God had promised, Isaac. Ismael was sent away because of Sarah's (formerly known as Sarai) jealousy. Now, in the 21st century, Ishmael and Isaac's ancestors still battle for their birthrights. Their choice is still impacting our world today.

I love the proverb, "When life gives you lemons, make lemonade" because it reminds us to make the best out of bad situations, but there are times when you don't need to make lemonade out of the lemons. You actually need to give them back. Many of our historical figures chose not to make the best out of their situation but rather to fight to change them. Dr. Martin Luther King dreamed of equality for all men, and he fought, nonviolently, for social change. He knew full well that this choice would cost his life, and it did, well before he died.

Rosa Parks was tired when she stepped on that bus, and I'm sure that tiredness was more than just being physically tired from work. I'm sure that in that moment, she was tired of having to make so many concessions as if she didn't matter. So, she continued to sit, knowing full well that she would be arrested or worse. Her choice was a pivotal point in the civil rights movement. They, along with countless others, fought tirelessly for us to enjoy our current freedom and equality. Yes, there is more work to be done but I am thankful that they were willing to sacrifice their present comfort for our future.

CHAPTER 2

CHOOSE A POSITIVE ATTITUDE

As a man thinketh in his heart so is he; — *Proverbs 23:7*

Attitude is defined as a settled way of thinking or feeling about someone or something, typically one that is reflected in one's behavior. We typically don't think about attitude until we cross paths with someone that has a bad one, but an attitude cannot be limited to an eye roll or rude statement because it is so much more than that. Attitude can also be referred to as a point of view or mindset.

Our attitude becomes the lens through which we view people, things, situations, ourselves and even God. It is possible for two people to look at the same dilemma and one sees it as manageable while the other sees it as impossible. Attitude is everything! It can make the heaviest of burdens easy to bear or it can make the easiest of burdens heavier to bear. There are some people who have what I call the "mole hill to mountain" ministry. The eternal pessimist, they are skilled at turning the most minor situation into a full-blown disaster.

Attitude plays a very important role in our ability to achieve success. Attitude can cause doors of opportunity to open for you. It can also cause doors that are open to close. Ability and intellect are important, but attitude is more important. Zig Ziglar puts it this way, "Your attitude, not your aptitude, will determine your altitude."

Having the right attitude makes 1 Thessalonians 5:18 possible: "In everything give thanks: for this is the will of God in Christ Jesus concerning you." If you are gloomy and depressed, you'll struggle to rejoice in anything. In Acts 16, Paul and Silas are beaten and thrown in jail for casting a spirit of divination out of a young girl. Over in the night, they started doing something that I'm sure seemed odd to the other prisoners.

And at midnight Paul and Silas prayed, and sang praises unto God: and the prisoners heard them. And suddenly there was a great earthquake, so that the foundations of the prison were shaken: and immediately all the doors were opened, and every one's bands were loosed. —Acts 16:25-26

That must've been some powerful prayer and praise! See, Paul and Silas knew what do in the midst of trouble; don't throw a pity party, throw a praise party. In Acts 5, Peter and the apostles are thrown in prison for preaching the gospel. God sends an angel to release them from prison and they go right back to preaching in the temple that they were arrested in. When the officers found them the next day and brought them before the counsel, they were beaten and told once more not to preach the gospel.

The apostles left the counsel rejoicing for having been found worthy to be punished for the gospel sake and went right back to teaching and preaching daily. You may be saying, "What does this have to do with attitude?" It has everything to do with attitude because how you see your opposition, determines how you will deal with it. When all hell breaks loose in your life- give thanks! When people talk about you or plot against you- give thanks!

You are not thanking God for the troubles, you are thanking him in the midst of them and in spite of them. If whining and complaining was going to fix your situation, then I would definitely recommend it but since it doesn't, go ahead and turn that whining into worship. Choose to do what Paul and Silas did, sing until the prison doors are open and the shackles are broken off your life.

See, Paul had already decided "... that the sufferings of this present time are not worthy to be compared to the glory which will be revealed" (Romans 8:18). The apostle's attitude about their sufferings was that it is worth it in order to further the kingdom.

What attitudes have you embraced towards the furtherance of the kingdom? Do you view it as being worth being talked about and criticized? Is it worth giving up some of your personal time and money? As preachers and teachers, we have to recognize that every sermon won't make you popular. And since this is not a popularity contest, you have to be okay when what God gives you to say ruffles some feathers.

There will be times when your lifestyle will cause people to dislike you but like the apostles, you have to consider it an honor when people come against you for doing what is right. But even if you should suffer for what is right, you are blessed. "Do not fear their threats; do not be frightened." But in your hearts revere Christ as Lord. Always be prepared to give an answer to everyone who asks you to give the reason for the hope that you have. But do this with gentleness and respect, keeping a clear conscience, so that those who speak maliciously against your good behavior in Christ may be ashamed of their slander.

For it is better, if it is God's will, to suffer for doing good than for doing evil. —1 Peter 3:14-17 NIV

Many of the children of Israel missed out on the promised land because of their negative attitudes toward God. Although, they had seen the many miracles that he had performed they still questioned his ability to take them to the promised land. Because of their whining and complaining, everyone over 20 except for Joshua and Caleb, died in the wilderness, having seen the promised land but never entering it (Numbers 14). What made Joshua and Caleb so special? Why were they the only two out of millions who would see the promise fulfilled?

Numbers 14:24 say's that Caleb had another spirit. Of the twelve spies sent to Canaan, Joshua and Caleb were the only two who believed what God said in spite of what their eyes had seen. They did not let the size of their opponent paralyze them. They knew that victory was theirs because God was with them. This is the attitude that we have to maintain throughout the ups and downs of our lives. Like Joshua and Caleb, we must learn to:

- Stand when others are falling. There will be times when you seem to be the last man standing but you have to stand anyway. Your ability to successfully complete the task assigned to you is not hinged on others' willingness to stand but rather on your own. The other ten spies had all but given up hope and their negative report caused everyone else to despair. But Joshua and Caleb held fast to their conviction that they were well able to conquer.

- Be encouraged when others are criticizing. The children of Israel were a very critical group of people. Although they had seen God work great miracles when they faced any obstacle they would immediately start to whine and complain. Although the complainers greatly outnumbered Joshua and Caleb, they managed to remain encouraged. There will be times when you have to encourage yourself. The best way to do that is by reading and meditating on the promises of God.

- Keep pushing forward. Joshua and Caleb were willing and ready to face whatever awaited them in the promise land. For them, the promise was greater than the obstacle that was blocking it. You have to keep pushing forward towards the promises of God. Sometimes the greatest obstacle that you will face is really not in front of you but behind. That's why Philippians 3:13-14 tells you to forget what is behind and press towards the mark. Since Joshua and Caleb were not swayed by the negative reports, the criticism nor by the mental image of all those who died in the wilderness, they were able to walk into what was promised them. Although it was 40 years later, they stayed the course and received the prize.

Your success hinges on your attitude. Those walls that separate you from the promises of God can and will come down as you keep the right attitude. When you keep your head in the right place God will give you a strategy to defeat the enemy. Learn to face your giants just as David faced Goliath. Run towards that obstacle with full assurance that the God that is in you is greater than anything that comes up against you. If he said it; that settles it.

Since an attitude is a settled way of thinking, we have to pay attention to what we are thinking about on a regular basis. We are bombarded with thoughts all day long, but we have to choose which ones we are going to allow to linger in our mind. Martin Luther puts it this way, "You cannot keep birds from flying over your head, but you can keep them from building a nest in your hair." We can't stop random thoughts from coming to mind, but we do not have to let them stay in our mind.

Pay attention to what is getting and keeping your thoughts. When you recognize that your thoughts are not wholesome and good then you have to give them an eviction notice. Bring your thought life into alignment with the word of God. The Law of Concentration say's that whatever you dwell on grows and expands in your life. Whatever you are focusing on today is what is being magnified in your life. Take a moment and consider what thoughts and ideas you have allowed to grow and expand in your life. Do they fit the description laid out for us in Philippians 4:8?

Finally, brethren, whatsoever things are true, whatsoever things are honest, whatsoever things are just, whatsoever things are pure, whatsoever things are lovely, whatsoever things are of good report; if there be any virtue, and if there be any praise, think on these things. —Philippians 4:8

If your thoughts about people, God, things, and yourself do not align with what the Bible says or how it says we ought to think, then we need to change our mind. We cannot live beyond the thoughts and idea that we embrace. Paul tells us in 2 Corinthians 10:4-5, "to use our weapons of warfare to cast down imaginations and to bring our thoughts into captivity." Whatever thoughts you allow to linger in your mind, good or bad, will began to direct your behavior.

If you want to change your life, you must change your thinking. Romans 12:2 tells us to be totally transformed by renewing our minds. The answer to most people's financial problem is not more money but rather transforming their minds where their finances are concerned and of course discipline. Giving a large sum of money to a spender just increases their opportunity to spend; it does not guarantee that they will pay down debts.

That's why I don't encourage debt consolidation. Consolidating debts creates extra money but if that person has not gotten a handle on their spending, they will eventually create more debt. If you do not change your way of thinking in the area in which you struggle, you will inevitably struggle in that area forever.

After getting saved, I realized there were so many places where I had to allow the word of God to transform my thinking. Here I was saved, sanctified, Holy Ghost filled, and fire baptized but dysfunctional. I didn't believe in paying my bills, but God sent me to every store that I owed money to work out a payment plan. I thought, as long as I financially supported my family I was doing good, but God had to teach me how to really be a father and a husband. Even as a pastor, I had to learn how to truly shepherd the sheep. Little by little God tore down every foolish thought and unhealthy tradition that I had embraced, then he built me back up into who He would have me to be. He changed my way of thinking and as a result transformed my entire life as well as that of my family.

You cannot have a positive attitude with a bad heart. Solomon, in Proverbs 4, tells us to guard our hearts because it is the source of life. If our heart is our life source, then what we allow to take root in our heart can either bless us or curse us. The One translation says that out of the heart is the 'wellspring of life.' If our heart is the wellspring of life, then it is vitally important that we keep the wellspring clean, or else what comes out of it will be contaminated.

None of us want to drink from a dirty well or fountain so why would you want to live out of one? The problem with a dirty wellspring is that eventually it will taint every aspect of your life. See, your failure to keep your heart pure will come out in your conversation. Sometimes it will be in barely recognizable slip ups here and there. Other times it will come out like a tsunami destroying everyone in its path. Luke 6:45 says, "Out of the abundance of the heart, the mouth speaks," meaning whatever we've allowed our hearts and minds to become full of is what is going to flow out of us.

When we don't guard against anger, jealousy and other negative emotions it becomes difficult to experience success in every arena. There are people who are successful in business, but they fail at family. There are those who are successful in their relationships, but they fail in business. Whole life success is possible when we make guarding our hearts a priority. I know some really talented and gifted people who are doing well but could be doing much better were it not for the unresolved issues in their heart that manifest in their behavior.

No matter how good things are, they have a way of self-sabotaging. We have to pay close attention to the thoughts and feelings that we are allowing to linger in our hearts and mind because the devil works hard to keep us vexed. Sometimes we are vexed with others and have to learn to quickly forgive just as God forgave us (Colossians 3:13). God doesn't make us go through twelve steps to gain forgiveness and He doesn't put us on a trial period to make sure we're worthy of His forgiveness. I once heard a quote that said, "Holding onto anger is like drinking poison expecting the other person to die." I'll say it again, forgive quickly. Then, refuse to allow the enemy to keep bringing the offense up even if you are the offender and the person that you are forgiving is yourself.

The attitudes that we choose to embrace can either bless or curse us. When we embrace the attitude of a conqueror then we will surely conquer and if we embrace the attitude of defeat, then we will surely be defeated. None of us can live beyond our attitudes. I want to encourage you just as God did Joshua in Joshua 1:6-8. "Be strong and courageous. Obey all the teaching given to you. Always remember what is written in the book (the Bible).

Study it day and night so that you can obey all that is in it. If you do this, you will be wise and successful in everything you do."

Don't be afraid because God is with you everywhere you go." Choose today, to start freeing yourself of every ill feeling and negative emotion. Give your heart permission to forget the pain of past failures and disappointments. Began filling your thoughts with good things, let your conversation be on the good things. If chaos ensues, put on strength because God is with you. If you can maintain a positive attitude through life's storms as well as when all is well then success is not just possible, but it is inevitable.

> *Be careful of your thoughts, for your thoughts become your words. Be careful of your words, for your words become your actions. Be careful of your actions, for your actions become your habits. Be careful of your habits, for your habits become your character. Be careful of your character, for your character becomes your destiny.* — Chinese proverb, author unknown

CHAPTER 3

CHOOSE YOUR INFLUENCES

He that walketh with wise men shall be wise: but a companion of fools shall be destroyed. —Proverbs 13:20

We have to choose wisely the company that we keep. There are warnings throughout the bible about bad company:

- Bad company corrupts good morals (I Corinthians 15:33).
- Don't sit with deceitful men (Psalms 26:4).
- Don't make friends with an angry man (Pro 22:24).

- Stay away from the path of the wicked (Proverbs 4:14).

Our companions have a profound influence on our choices. God warned the Israelites to keep their distance from the people that worshiped other gods. He told them not to intermarry with them nor to let their children marry them. Their choice to ignore God's warnings eventually led to their downfall. They chose evil companions that influenced them, and that bad influence led to their abandonment of God. God's warnings about our companions are still in effect. He doesn't tell us things to hurt us. He tells us things to help us.

When He speaks of choosing our companions wisely, He does so because He knows that bad company ruins good manners (I Corinthians 15:33) and will lead us away from the blessed life. By that same token, when we are in fellowship with good people, who are doing good things it has a way of rubbing off on us. We need people in our lives that challenge us to do and be better, whether it's by what they say or by how they live. Proverbs 27:17 says, "that your friends should sharpen you and make you better."

Choose your inner circle wisely. These are the people who will influence you most. If you're a young adult reading this, I want you to pay close attention to this because I have seen countless young adults leave their parents' home and start hanging with the wrong crowd. Some of them come back home, others wish they could and then there are those who are home, but their lives are forever changed.

Tell me who you run with and I'll tell you what you are going to be like because you become like those you closely associate with. If you hang around people long enough, you pick up their habits, whether they are good or bad. This is especially important for young adult entering college. You are going to be surrounded by all kinds of people, some with healthy and wholesome lifestyles, others who are constantly "turnt up". You have to decide which group you're going to hang with. It is impossible to be on the scene for every party, club and other event and it not affect your mind, health and even your grades.

Let me encourage you to stay away from the party scene and definitely stay away from drugs and alcohol. Drugs and alcohol will lower your inhibitions and lowered inhibitions can lead to careless and immoral decisions as well as devastating life consequences. You have to settle the issue of drugs and alcohol before you are faced with the choice.

Another issue that needs to be settled is that of premarital sex. God designed sex to take place between two adults married to each other and you have to determine in your heart before someone is blowing in your ear that you're going to live by God's standard. People want the benefit of marriage without the commitment and whether you know it or not, casually partaking in the act creates a tie (a soul tie) that should be reserved for husband and wife.

I knew of a young man who became very angry with his girlfriend when she gave her life to the LORD and put the brakes on their physical relationship. Moving forward, she decided to save sex for marriage and he was upset. Ladies, if a man will not honor you and treat you like a lady, don't look at him!

Let me tell you something, if you require that a man will respect you and treat you like a lady, he will swim the widest sea and cross the hottest desert just for you. Don't be afraid to set Godly standards. If you lose someone- male or female- because of your standards, then he or she is not the one that God has for you.

Speaking of the one that God has for you, you have to choose wisely who you will date and marry. I know during the dating phase that the bees are swarming but fan the bees away and ask the important questions: Are you a believer? What exactly do you believe? Are you active in your church? Do you have a job? Is there anything in your bank account? The list goes on and on... If you are in a serious dating relationship, do not be afraid to ask the uncomfortable questions.

It's better to know on the front end what you are getting into and if you really want to get into it. I encourage singles not to "missionary date." That means dating someone who has no interest in God while convincing yourself that you are going to get him or her saved. If they are not saved, then they are not currently a candidate for you, as a believer, to marry so don't entangle your heart. Going to church does not equal saved. You have to have a real and active relationship with God. Don't buy into the notion that a piece of a man is better than no man at all. That idea is one of a lowered expectation. Ladies, get busy serving God and He will send Boaz across your path and you will know its him because he will be a God-fearing man who is trustworthy, honorable, and courageous. He will be an earnest worker in whatever his chosen profession is and a champion for those less fortunate.

He will be a tithe payer and a seed sower and will honor and esteem you highly. Brothers, you will recognize Ruth because she will be the one diligently working and serving others not trying to get attention or preferential treatment. She'll be honorable, nurturing and the genuine- one, in whom your heart can safely trust. The mate that you choose can greatly bless your life or they can greatly hinder your life so choose wisely.

Choosing what information, we will ingest is just as important as choosing who we will allow in our lives. With almost everyone in possession of a smart phone, tablet or computer, everything is easily accessible. Movies, music and all venues of entertainment are available on our gadgets. Are you listening to music that encourages poor morals, vulgarity and hatred? Are you watching shows and movies filled with violence, filthy language and sexual content? Would you feel comfortable sitting next to Jesus, listening to what you are listening to or watching what you are watching.

We have to pay attention to what we give our attention to. If "we are what we eat" in terms of food, then the same can be said of what we eat in terms of information. A few years back, I had to stop watching the news. We were in the middle of an economic crisis and the more I watched, the more I feared. I started believing the report of the news analyst over the report of the Lord. I had to change the information I was constantly taking in so that I could change my conversation.

If your mind is constantly bombarded with negativity and ungodliness, it will begin to show in your conversation, lifestyle and appetites. If you surround yourself with what is good and wholesome, that too will begin to show in your conversation, lifestyle and appetite. I want to encourage you to pay special attention to the word of God. It is designed to teach us, correct us and to train us in righteousness (2 Timothy 3:16). Plus, all of the blessings found in the word of God are ours for the asking. But being in church is not enough, you have to actually hear what is said.

Mark 4:24 tells us to pay attention to what we hear because the measure of attention we give it, determines how it will be able to produce in our lives. If you want to enjoy the blessed life, you have to choose wisely who and what you allow to influence you.

Psalms 119:66 says, "Teach me good judgement and knowledge; for I have believed thy commandments."

We have to begin exercising good judgement in all areas of life and not give ourselves a scape goat when good judgement is not exercised. We listen to crazy music and live crazy lives and attempt to chalk it up to "culture". No, it's not culture, it's a choice and we have to start choosing better.

How many accidents have resulted from someone choosing to respond to a text while driving? How many lives have been taken because someone impaired by alcohol decided to drive? How many people have flunked out or been kicked out of college because of wild partying? How many people have ended up totally backsliding because they chose to dabble in things that God had delivered them from? I'll leave you with this quote from Colin Powell:

> "With some people you spend an evening: with others you invest it. 'Wise is the person who fortifies his life with the right friendships. If you run with wolves, you will learn how to howl. But, if you associate with eagles, you will learn how to soar to great heights."

CHAPTER 4

CHOOSING TO HONOR

Every day we are faced with making some type of choices. We must choose what to wear, what to buy, what to watch on TV, or what to read or what to eat or drink. The list never ends. Our lives consist of all types of choices every day. Although most of our lives are on autopilot, we must remind ourselves to pay attention to the choices we make; they can and do affect the quality of our lives.

Since God allows us to choose, then we ought to choose wisely. Our destiny is shaped by the choices we make, not by the circumstances that comes our way. If we want to have a different outcome for our lives, then we must make better choices.

Choosing to honor is one of the best decisions that we can make to improve the quality of our own lives. To have high respect, great esteem or the highest regard for another means that we must (1 Peter 2:17) honor all people, love the brotherhood, fear God, and honor the king. The idea of honoring others comes, especially those in authority, from the fact that they represent God's ultimate authority. When we honor, we honor God.

Honoring is so essential in our life that God put in the bible for us to honor our father and our mother so that things may be well with us in the earth. Honoring our parents is one of the Ten Commandments that include a promise from God of a long life. Honoring is an inward attitude of high esteem with words and actions that demonstrates the respect one may have for another. Children should respect parents, even if they don't really deserve it, because God said it. In essence, when we pay our respect to our parents we are actually doing the commandment that God established for all generations (Exodus 20:12).

While obeying with words, actions will reveal the real motive. When this principle is implemented early in life while still in youth, it will become a habit or way of life for that individual. After maturity, the obedience that children learn will serve them in honoring authorities such as government, police, and employers. Parents chose to bring children into the world, therefore we should choose to honor parents.

We are to honor parents in righteousness only and not to imitate nor follow nor carry out ungodly acts or instructions (Ezekiel 20:18-19). If an ungodly parent instructs a child to do something that contradicts God commands, that child must obey God rather than his/her parents (Acts 5:29). Honoring is not always easy nor is it always fun, but it's necessary to reap the benefits that God promised.

Let every soul be subject to the governing authorities (Roman 13:1). The Office of the President is a good example of how we are to respect the rank of those in leadership, even from the world standpoint. We don't always agree with who is in the office, nor their decisions, but we should honor the leader of this country. Whenever the Democratic Party wins the office, the Republicans are not pleased and vice versa, but we should honor the authority of the position.

Obey your leaders and submit to them (Roman 13:17). Respecting Bishops, Pastors, Elders and leaders was instituted by God for spiritual governing authority. They watch over your souls and will have to give an account.

The church is a place that should be consecrated, or considered holy ground, and should be treated as such. As we enter into the premises, just as in biblical days we should regard the church as God's dwelling place. Yes, we are aware that God dwells in the heart of believers, but the right mindset upon entering our place of worship shall honor other believers. Respect and honor should be given to the White House and any place of authority.

If you want to be honored, you must choose to honor others. It's a simple principle of sowing and reaping. God will not honor those who will not honor. Honor everyone (I Peter 2:17).

CHAPTER 5

CHOOSE SUCCESSFUL HABITS

Behind every successful person there is a pattern of good choices. I'm sure there are some bad choices back there too, but in order for any of us to truly be successful we have to begin forming successful habits. A habit is a settled or regular tendency or practice especially one that is hard to break. Successful habits will bring favorable outcomes. For a moment, let's examine a few habits that will lead us to success:

1. Choose to Keep Dreaming.

God revealed his purpose and plan for Joseph's life through a dream. That dream, tattooed on his heart and mind, is what sustained him in the pit, in prison and in the palace. Joseph never stopped dreaming and he held fast to what God had shown him, even when others were displeased with him.

There have been many occasions in which my wife and I could have thrown in the towel. The pits in life can overwhelm any of us but we must keep dreaming continually holding fast to what God has shown us and what he has said concerning us. When opposition comes or doubt rears its ugly head, you must choose to continue moving forward in what you know. Well, what if all hell breaks loose? The old saints would say "tie a knot in the rope and hold on!" If you are in the proverbial pit today, know that your dreams are there to sustain you just as they did for Joseph. They are there to encourage you to keep forging ahead knowing that what is ahead of you is much greater than what's behind.

2. Choose Passion Over Passivity

It could easily be said of David that he was a passionate man. He ran towards Goliath when those who were trained in battle were shaking in their boots (1 Samuel 17). When the ark of the covenant was brought home, David danced out of his royal garments in honor and celebration of God (2 Samuel 6). Even God referred to him as "a man after his own heart". David was in constant pursuit of God and he gave his all to every task. David chose passion over passivity. Passion, when pointed towards a noble cause, can be an energizing force for good.

When you are passionate about something "that'll do" actually won't do anymore. Your aim won't be to just complete the job but rather to do it well and to do it right. Passion is what keeps some people up late working towards an expected end and it is what sends others to bed early so that they can rise early for that same purpose. Let passion be the fuel that drives you forward when others have stopped moving and pursuing. It will take the work out of your work and turn your obligations into opportunities.

3. Choose God-Confidence Over Self- Confidence

Cultivating a God-confidence means training yourself to view yourself through the lens of the word instead of the lens of the world. The world teaches self-reliance based solely on your abilities, and connections that bring about success. Meanwhile, the word teaches God-reliance, which is based on God's power working through our abilities and sometimes merely our availability, creating connections and opportunities that bring us to success.

Yes, we should believe in ourselves, but we should believe in God more. According to Philippians 4:13, we can do all things through Christ who strengthens us, and when we feel like we can't or we face something that we can't conquer on our own, we recognize that God's strength is made perfect in our weakness (2 Corinthians 12:9).

4. Know Your Personal Limitations

In his prayer at Gideon, Solomon spoke of himself as a little child (I King 3) not knowing how to go in and out amongst the people. Solomon knew that he was charting unfamiliar territory therefore, mistakes were bound to happen. He knew that he needed further instruction. So, he decided to lean on the one who knows all and who he could go to for wisdom. Like Solomon, we have to be just as aware of our limitations as we are of our strengths.

We also have to know that our limitations do not have to limit our life. Most of us, at some time have said to someone to "stay in your lane" and although people often take offence to the statement, there is some wisdom in it. Staying in your lane simply means working in the area that you are best suited or skilled for. Some of our greatest mistakes are made when we attempt to do what someone else is doing and we are simply not gifted in that area.

I have been blessed to minister alongside some giants in the gospel. Many of them are more educated than I am and have been blessed to accomplish great things. But none of this makes me inferior. My lack of a formal education may be one of my personal limitations, but it has in no way limited my life because by the grace of God, I too, have been blessed to do great things. I have enjoyed collaborating with other preachers of the gospel, learning from them and even speaking into their lives. Our limitations are nothing more than opportunities for growth and collaboration- we collaborate with God and others to accomplish things and in the process, we grow as individuals and oftentimes improve in an area where improvement is needed.

5. Choose to Plan

Now that you've got some things in your heart that you want to accomplish, what do you do next? I believe the next step is to plan. There's an old Proverb that says, "He who fails to plan is planning to fail". Without making some plans and provisions for your life you are inevitably leaving your life to chance. "Que sera, sera, whatever will be, will be" may have been a hit song for Doris Day, but it cannot be the anthem for our lives. We must sit still long enough to seek the counsel of God and sometimes others in order to get a game plan for our lives.

Planning keeps us from being all over the place while accomplishing little. It allows us to be strategic in our efforts and in doing so, we get the most out of our time spent on any task. When we plan we give ourselves an opportunity to celebrate the small victories along the way checking off each task when completed.

For which of you, intending to build a tower, sitteth not down first, and counteth the cost, whether he have sufficient to finish it? Lest haply, after he hath laid the foundation, and is not able to finish it, all that behold it begin to mock him, Saying, This man began to build, and was not able to finish.—Luke 14:28-30

We don't want to be like those, who set out to do great things and fizzle out midstream laying foundations but never finishing anything. Get a plan then work the plan knowing that when you commit your works to the Lord, your thoughts and plans will be established.

6. Hear Both Sides Before Choosing

Whether you are making a decision on a personal matter or one that is between others, making a decision with limited information is not wise. Proverbs 11:14 says that safety is found in the multitude of counsellors and that's not because they all agree but because they have the ability to see one situation from different perspectives. Solomon exercised the principle when having to judge between two mothers; one of which whose baby had died.

Solomon was able to discern who the rightful mother was by presenting them with what would have been a difficult choice which was to cut the baby in half. He knew that the birth mother would rather give up her right to her child than to see the child cut in half. When we settle down and slow down long enough to hear all sides of a given situation, we position ourselves to better discern the best course of action. God is always speaking.

7. Succeed at Being You

As a young minister I began mimicking the older more experienced preachers that I was around. I tried grabbing my ear and squalling like the Pastor at my home church and later I started preaching like the Pastors and ministers that I was in association with. I was trying to preach what others told me to preach, how they told me to preach, and because of this, I ended up losing myself in the process. I had no clue of who I was as a preacher and I didn't know what my message was. Had I continued on that path I would have been miserable.

But I chose to really seek to know God for myself, to know what He wanted me to preach, and to know how He wanted me to preach it. If I was going to be effective in the kingdom, I had to be me and if you are going to be effective in life, you must be you! Your success is rooted in trusting the YOU that God created you to be. Psalm. 37:37 tells us to mark the perfect man, meaning to take notice of him, or to pay attention to how he lives. We learn from the lives of others. By their successes and their failures, but even so, we should never try to become them.

Years ago, I stopped one of my leaders from saying "fake it till you make it" to the congregation. Although I understood the message she was trying to convey, God reminded me that we are not called to be fake, we should be the real deal! If all our effort went into looking like something we weren't then we would not have to put so much effort into becoming what we ought to be.

We owe it to our God who fearfully and wonderfully made us (Psalm. 139:14) to be who He has created us to be. He has cataloged every detail about us; even the number of hairs on our head (Luke 12:7), and He makes no mistakes. He has a plan for our lives and it is to prosper us and bring us to an expected end (Jeremiah. 29:11). We are always on God's mind (Psalm 8:4) and he has good works planned for us to walk in (Ephesians 2:10).

CHAPTER 6

CHOOSE WISDOM- MAKE IT YOUR OBSESSION

Wisdom is the principal thing; therefore, get wisdom: and with all thy getting get understanding. — Proverbs 4:7

Of all the things that we pursue in life, there is one that is of the utmost importance and that is wisdom. Wisdom is such a valuable commodity in the life of the believer that Solomon refers to it as a woman and tell us to "get her" because she is the principal thing. Principal by definition is the first in order of importance. So, Solomon is literally telling us that wisdom is the first in order of importance, so get her.

Throughout scripture we often see wisdom, knowledge and understanding intertwined with one another so I want to briefly explain all three. Knowledge is defined as facts, information, and skills acquired by a person through experience or education. Simply put, knowledge is what you know or have learned. Understanding, on the other hand, is getting the meaning out of your knowledge and knowing the choices that are available. Principles for living are formed through what we understand.

Wisdom gives you the correct application of knowledge and understanding. It will also help you know which principle to apply to a given situation. It is possible to be knowledgeable and not have understanding and wisdom. There are a lot of smart-dummies out there. I call them smart-dummies because although they are highly educated and know a great deal, they lack the understanding and wisdom to take what they know and build a good life.

Charles Spurgeon put it this way, "Wisdom is the right use of knowledge. To know is not to be wise. Many men know a great deal and are greater fools for it. There is no fool so great a fool as a knowing fool. But to know how to use knowledge is to have wisdom." We need all three: knowledge, understanding and wisdom, working together to produce a successful life.

"Through wisdom is an house builded; and by understanding it is established: And by knowledge shall the chambers be filled with all precious and pleasant riches." — Proverbs 24:3

Wisdom becomes the foundation on which we build but not just any wisdom but skillful, godly wisdom. So often we are trying to build on what we know alone. We lay our foundation for businesses, family and life on our abilities, our connections and our knowledge, but God wants us to build on a firmer foundation. That foundation is Him: His knowledge, His connections, His abilities through us. Wisdom is the principle thing, it's first in order of importance. That means getting the wisdom of God before you get the wife or husband.

Getting the wisdom of God before you start the business or purchase a home. Get wisdom first! What a mess we make when we set out to do great things without seeking the wisdom of God. Oftentimes we refuse to sit down with any wise counsel. James 1:5 says "If any of you lack wisdom, let him ask of God, that giveth to all men liberally, and upbraideth not; and it shall be given him." If you are in need of wisdom today, my prayer is that you would go to the One who knows all, understands all, and is wiser than all. He is waiting on you. He is invested in your success, so He waits for the opportunity to help you.

Understanding will establish you. It will establish your going and establish your doing. Understanding will organize your efforts and it will help you to better respond to what you see with wisdom. Finally, through knowledge, we can fill every space with precious and pleasant riches. Some riches will come in the form of money, others in the form of connections and opportunities. As I stated earlier, we need all three of these working together to produce a successful life.

When pride comes [boiling up with an arrogant attitude of self-importance], then come dishonor and shame, But with the humble [the teachable who have been chiseled by trial and who have learned to walk humbly with God] there is wisdom and soundness of mind. —Proverbs 11:2 Amp

We have to recognize that wisdom hangs out with the humble. When you see someone who is proud and boastful, you can rest assured that he or she does not have the wisdom of God. The humble recognize their total dependence on God. They recognize that He alone is the creator and that we are the creation, so they eagerly look for the opportunity to sit at His feet and learn. Even if they are educated, they know that His knowledge far exceeds theirs; their knowledge is limited whiles His is limitless.

The humble listen for His voice, His leading, His direction while the proud says to himself "I know what to do." Though the proud may be successful, imagine the level of success they could experience if they would've included God in their plans. In Numbers 12:3-8, Moses is described as "very

THE POWER OF CHOICE • 55

meek, above all the men which were upon the face of the earth", and God says of him, "With him I speak mouth to mouth [directly}, clearly and openly and not in riddles;" (Amplified).

This is the relationship that God wants with us today, but we will only experience it through humility. Paul says in Philippians 3:7, "But what things were gain to me, I counted as loss for Christ." He closes out verse 8 with, "...I have suffered the loss of all things, and do count them but dung, that I may win Christ..." Listen, Paul was a highly educated man, but he recognized that what he had learned without God was nothing compared to what he was learning with Him. Now, I don't want you thinking that I have an issue with having an education. By all means, get an education, we need skilled and knowledgeable people in the body of Christ. Just make sure that you get the wisdom of God because it is the principle thing.

Neither me nor my wife have a college degree but with the help of God we have managed to secure a very comfortable life, and by very comfortable, I mean we are BLESSED!

If I am bragging, I'm bragging on God because he took an old country boy and girl from the wrong side of the track, saved them and cleaned them up really good. Then He gave them wisdom and an avenue and they have been working it ever since. Humility was easy for us because we were broke but I have found that some of the most prideful people you'll ever meet are broke people. Let me encourage you with 1 Peter 5:6, "Humble yourselves therefore, under the mighty hand of God, that he may exalt you in due time." Be humble and seek the wisdom of God. When your "due time" comes, no devil in hell or person on earth will be able to stop it.

One area where the body Christ needs to choose wisdom is in the area of finance. As preachers we've been telling the saints that "when the praises go up, the blessings come down." They have been praising and shouting and many are still struggling. That is not the will of God for His children. He is a good Father and does not want to see his children suffer. Our God delights in our prosperity (Psalms 35:27) so why aren't we prospering?

I can remember praying for other's finances and God quickly moving for them while my wife and I still struggled. I even questioned God about that and His response was to give me a message on debt-free living. My wife didn't believe it was possible but once she got on board, we started doing exactly what God said. The first thing He told us to do was "Stop spending." We shut down for years, only buying what was necessary. My wife was feeding a family of five with $20 per week!

The next thing He told us was to start paying off our debts and we did. During this season there was no extra money because every penny had a purpose. Lastly, we had to learn to love saving more than spending. My wife sold Amway. We have owned burger joints and flipped houses. We worked every avenue that was available to ensure that we would not be in a tight financial situation forever. By 1997, we were completely debt free. Our home, cars and even our children were paid for! We were able to conquer our debt and get in better control of our finances through skillful and Godly wisdom and hard work.

Wisdom won't work if you don't work. We don't want to be like the man who saved the city, but no one remembered him because he was poor (Ecclesiastes 9:13-15). Whether we like it or not, people typically don't want to hear a broke man. If we are going to be effective in the kingdom and our communities, we have to have a voice that people will hear. Don't allow your unwillingness to grow in the area of finance to cause you to lose your influence. God is looking for people that He can trust to be His distribution centers.

These are people that He can trust to feed the hungry, clothe the naked and to financially support the working of the kingdom. Matthew 24:45 asks the question, "Who is the faithful and wise servant, whom the master has put in charge of the servants in his household to give them their food at the proper time?" Are you a faithful and wise servant, whom God can put in charge? If not, it's high time that you become one. Get the wisdom of God for every area of your life, including your money.

It's hard to talk about wisdom and it's benefits without talking about Solomon. One humble prayer at Gibeon asking for wisdom and understanding, instead of riches and fame positioned him to not only be the wisest man to ever live but also the richest.

God gave Solomon wisdom and very great insight, and a breadth of understanding as measureless as the sand on the seashore. —I King 4:29

With wisdom came honor. The wisdom of Solomon caused him to gain honor throughout the nations. 1 King 4:30 says that people from all nations came to listen to Solomon's wisdom, sent by all the kings. The Queen of Sheba, having heard of Solomon's wisdom came to test him with hard questions and he was able to answer every question and nothing was difficult for him. She was amazed.

And when the queen of Sheba had seen all Solomon's wisdom, and the house that he had built, And the meat of his table, and the sitting of his servants, and the attendance of his ministers, and their apparel, and his cupbearers, and his ascent by which he went up unto the house of the LORD; there was no more spirit in her. —1 King 10: 4-5

Overwhelmed by Solomon's wisdom, riches, the excellence of his house and servants, the Queen of Sheba fainted. She recognized that everything she had heard was true, but it still paled in comparison to what she was seeing and experiencing (1 King 10:6-9). Solomon gained honor throughout all the nations because of wisdom. Let's take a look at Daniel, whose wisdom and insight brought him to a place of honor. When no one could interpret the dream of the King in Daniel chapter 2, he prayed to God for the interpretation. He received the interpretation and was promoted in the king's court. Later in chapter 5, when the astrologers and magicians could not interpret the writing written on the wall by a hand that appeared, Daniel was once more summoned. His wisdom in interpreting the writing caused him to be promoted to the third highest ruler in the kingdom.

Finally let's look at Joseph whose interpretation of a dream not only brought him to a place of honor but his wisdom positioned Egypt to flourish when all around them the land was in a famine. In Genesis 37, Joseph is sold into slavery by his brothers. He finds favor in the eyes of his master, Potiphar, and is put over all of his house. But when his wife accuses him of trying to sleep with her, he is thrown into prison (Chapter 39). While in prison he interprets the dream of a baker and a cupbearer (Chapter 40), which positions him to be called on to interpret the King's dream in chapter 41. Since, seven years of plenty were coming followed by seven years of severe famine, Joseph tells Pharaoh to appoint discerning and wise men over the land of Egypt and Pharaoh appoints him (Genesis 41:29-40).

Joseph wisely stores a fifth of the harvest during the seven years of plenty so that when the famine came, Egypt did not feel its affect. When his brothers came seeking for food to feed their family, Joseph was not overcome with bitterness but recognized that he was on assignment from God (Genesis 45:5-8). These three, gained honor through wisdom. They were able to strategically use what they had learned and experienced as well as the spiritual gifting they were given and it positioned them to rise in rank in their respective places and kingdoms.

"I, wisdom, dwell together with prudence; I possess knowledge and discretion. To fear the LORD is to hate evil; I hate pride and arrogance, evil behavior and perverse speech. Counsel and sound judgment are mine; I have insight, I have power. By me kings reign and rulers issue decrees that are just; by me princes govern, and nobles—all who rule on earth. I love those who love me, and those who seek me find me. With me are riches and honor, enduring wealth and prosperity. My fruit is better than fine gold; what I yield surpasses choice silver. I walk in the way of righteousness, along the paths of justice, bestowing a rich inheritance on those who love me and making their treasuries full." — Proverbs 8:12-21

CONCLUSION

As you see, the pages that we have covered contains a powerful message about how choices that we make influence the nature of life that we lead. Both in the relationship between God and us, as well as between ourselves as humans, God gave given us the ability to choose. My prayer is that you exercise the right choices and to have consideration of how your choices will impact on your lifestyles. Making the right choice about our behaviors, the company that we keep and how we treat others significantly impacts whether we will live a full life with blessings or otherwise.

I have shown you with the word of God how significant the power of choice truly is. This message is relevant in today's society where we are faced with so many choices. It is becoming more necessary that we learn the importance of making the right choices if we are to survive in a world that is becoming more and more distracted from the message of God.

ABOUT THE AUTHOR

Bishop Connie Wright is a native of Fayette County in Tennessee. He was born to the union of Allen and Thelma Wright. He was united in holy matrimony to his high school sweetheart, Annie Wright, and is the natural father of four.

Bishop Wright was ordained a minister under the leadership of Reverend Houston at Springhill Missionary Baptist church. He later served as an Associate Minister to Pastor Elvin Jones and worked diligently with the Somerville Branch of Bountiful Blessings. As a young minister, Bishop Wright spent a great deal of his time hosting tent revivals and bible studies in Fayette and surrounding Counties.

He founded House of Faith True Holiness Church in May 1987. During this time, services were held in the Somerville Community Center with only seven people in attendance. The church eventually moved into a former auto parts store which had been renovated by

Bishop Wright. Eventually the church name was changed to House of Faith Ministries.

In 1993, Bishop Wright began the Walk of Faith radio broadcast on WOJG 94.7 in Bolivar, Tennessee. This broadcast still airs Monday through Friday at 12 noon. Later that year, the doors of the Bolivar location of House of Faith Ministries were opened.

As the membership grew, so did the need for a bigger sanctuary. Having purchased land on the north end of town, Bishop Wright and the Mighty Men of Valor built a sanctuary. That sanctuary was destroyed by fired in late 1999. In January 2001, the doors of House of Faith Ministries Family Life Center opened for service.

Called to establish churches, Bishop Wright planted another church in Alamo, Tennessee. Services began on Friday Nights and were later changed to Sunday Morning as a new Pastor was installed. Under his leadership House of Faith is blessed to occupy its current sanctuary debt-free.

A community activist, Bishop Wright started the Maximizing Your Life Mentorship Program for teens. He has come alongside the Fayette County Schools system in many of their endeavors. He and the Mighty Men of Valor started Hope Outreach - a community initiative that renovates homes and provides other support to the community. He and his wife also work with the Justice System to provide temporary housing to women who are displaced or recently released from jail. The Pathway House is still providing shelter from the storms of life.

INDEX

A

abilities, 2, 13, 17–18, 43, 47, 52, 63
anger, 6, 24–25
attention, 20, 32–34, 36, 48
attitude, 2, 12–13, 15–17, 19–20, 25
authority, 37–39

B

believers, 31–32, 39, 50
blessings, 2, 5–7, 9, 34, 56, 63

C

celebration, 42
change, 10, 21–22, 33
children, 5–6, 9, 17–18, 28, 37–38, 56–57
choices, 2–3, 5–11, 28, 30, 35–36, 47, 51, 63
choosing, 2–3, 5, 28, 32, 35, 37, 47
church, 8, 31–32, 34, 39, 65–66
commandments, 5–6, 37
connections, 43, 52–53
conversation, 8, 23, 26, 33–34

counsellors, 47
culture, 35
curses, 5, 23, 25

D

debt, 6, 22, 57
destiny, 26, 36
direction, 54
disappointments, 26
discern, 47
dishonor, 54
disobedience, 9
dream, 40–41, 60–61
dreaming, 3, 41

E

earth, 5, 37, 55–56, 62
education, 51, 55
enemy, 20, 25
equality, 10–11

F

failures, 6, 23, 26, 49
faith, 9, 66
famine, 60–61

fools, 27, 52
forgive, 25

G

generations, 9, 37
God, 2–10, 13–17, 19–22, 25–26, 28, 30–32, 35–43, 45, 47–49, 52–61, 63–64
guard, 23–24

H

habits, 26, 29, 38, 40
heart, 12, 23–24, 30, 32, 39, 41, 45
heart permission, 26
Holy Ghost, 22
home, 6, 9, 29, 42, 53, 57
honor, 3, 16, 30, 32, 36–39, 42, 59–62
honoring, 37–38
humility, 55–56

I

improvement, 45
information, 32–33, 51
inheritance, 62
inhibitions, 30
instructions, 5, 38, 44

J

jealousy, 10, 24

K

kingdom, 8, 15–16, 48, 58, 60–61
knowledge, 3–4, 9, 34, 51–54, 62

L

leaders, 38–39, 49
leadership, 38, 65
lessons, 2–3
lifestyles, 16, 29, 33–34, 63
limitations, 44–45
love, 5–6, 10, 37, 62

M

marriage, 30
mindset, 2, 12
ministers, 44, 48, 59, 65
miracles, 17
money, 16, 22, 53, 58
morals, 3, 33

N

nations, 59–60

O

obligations, 42
obsession, 3, 50
obstacle, 18–20
opposition, 15, 41

P

parents, 29, 37–38
passion, 3, 41–42
passionate, 2, 41–42
passivity, 3, 41–42
perspectives, 47
plans, 40, 45–46, 49, 54
power, 43, 62–63
praise, 14, 21
prayer, 14, 43, 53, 63
preach, 14, 48
preachers, 16, 45, 48, 56
pride, 54
prison, 14, 41, 61
promises, 10, 17, 19, 37
prosperity, 2, 56, 62

prosperous life, 5

R

relationship, 3, 24, 31, 55, 63
riches, 53, 59–60, 62
righteousness, 34, 38, 62

S

sanctuary, 66
season, 57
self-confidence, 3, 43
self-importance, 54
self-reliance, 43
self-sabotaging, 24
servants, 58–60
sin, 7–9
situation, 10, 13, 15, 47, 51
Solomon, 23, 43–44, 47, 50, 58–60
spies, 6–7, 17–18
spiritual gifting, 61
storms, 67
sufferings, 2, 15

T

teachers, 16

thinking, 2, 12, 20–23, 55
thoughts, 20–21, 24, 26, 46
time, 15, 44, 46, 56, 58, 65
trust, 32, 58

U

understanding, 4, 50–53, 59
ungodliness, 33

V

victories, 17, 46

W

walls, 19, 60
wilderness, 17, 19
wisdom, 3–4, 44, 50–54, 56, 58–62
words, 26, 37, 43

www.ingramcontent.com/pod-product-compliance
Lightning Source LLC
Chambersburg PA
CBHW071538080526
44588CB00011B/1710